COUNTRY AND BLUES HARMONICA FOR THE MUSICALLY HOPELESS

COUNTRY & BLUES
HARMONICA
for the
Musically Hopeless

by Jon Gindick
illustrated by Barry Geller

KLUTZ®

Illustrations © by Barry Geller
Published by Klutz₍ᵣ₎ Palo Alto, California
Printed in the United States of America

Write Us
Klutz is an independent publisher located in
Palo Alto, California, and staffed entirely by real
human beings. We would love to hear your
comments regarding this or any of our books.

KLUTZ₍ᵣ₎
455 Portage Avenue
Palo Alto, CA 94306

Additional Copies
For the location of your nearest Klutz retailer, call
(605) 857-0888. Should they be tragically out of stock,
additional copies of this book, as well as the entire
library of "100% Klutz certified" books, are available
in our mail order catalogue. See back page.

ISBN 0-932592-08-2

4 1 5 4 2 4 0 7 3

The "book and bag" packaging
format is a registered
trademark
of Klutz

"Deep in the soul of every man, woman and child beats the heart of a frustrated harmonica player—or at least I *hope* so . . ."

The Author

Contents

I BOUGHT MY FIRST harmonica when I was 16 years old. It was a tinny wonder with a little picture of a cowboy and a hobo on the box. A regular $2.75 squeaker.

But I didn't care. I had music burning in my soul.

I spent hours listening to records and trying to play along. I polished a rendition of *O Susannah* that could set off every dog on my street and the next. *Old Folks at Home* was my next victim, followed by *Camptown Races*.

And that's where I stayed. For months.

I didn't know it at the time, but I was trapped in the "Third-Day-to-Forever" syndrome. I'd been playing for nearly a year when a friend, in desperation, pointed out that I hadn't learned a thing since about 3 days after I'd bought my harp.

The truth hurts.

He was right, of course, I had my 3 tunes, but what I didn't have was that ... sound ... that wailing, late night, talk-to-me kind of sound that led me to shell out my allowance in the first place.

How did you get that?

I re-read the back of the box and the little flier inside. Blow on the 2 hole. Draw on the 1 hole. *Dooh-dah. Dooh-dah.*

Not much help there.

I can't remember the moment, it must have been somewhere around the 6,000th rendition of *Old Folks at Home,* when I made *The Discovery.* For a fleeting bluesy moment, my harmonica sang to me in a whole new voice—Cross Harp style.

And suddenly, it was a brand new ballgame.

What you've got in your hand, I modestly believe, can save you and your friends a great deal of *Camptown Races* time. The secret to country and blues harmonica is something I learned the hard way, but I have since taught it to hundreds of students with a great deal less frustration.

And I'm not talking about musicians. I'm talking about the tone-deaf multitudes. The tin-ear contingent, the piano lesson drop-outs, The Hopeless Ones. For them, I'm their final effort, their Musical Last Chance.

And, as a teacher of harmonica, I've never been stumped.

If you can talk, you can play harmonica. You use your breath, vocal chords, mouth, lips, tongue and sense of rhythm to make sounds that communicate. It's the same with harmonica—only easier. Not many people can make one word repeated over and over into a very interesting conversation. But I can show you how to turn on a one-note blues jam that'll have you stomping your foot in no time.

The idea is to get you jamming along with the music on the cassette today. You've got everything you need—book, tape, harmonica and musical soul. So put your tape in a recorder, pull your harmonica out of its box, and let's get going.

CHAPTER
ONE
The Tools of Your Trade

Your Pocket Pal Harmonica

Meet M. Hohner's marvelous musical invention, the ten hole, diatonic harmonica. Herr Hohner originally designed his reed instrument to play German waltzes and polka music in 1877. But that was before it crossed the Atlantic and met with the Afro-American blues sound.

You'll notice that your new friend's holes are numbered. Hold the harmonica (once the two of you become a little better acquainted, you can call it a "harp"), with the numbers facing up. You'll see the letter "C" engraved on the metal plating, indicating this instrument is built to play in the key of "C". Do you understand what this means?

No? Good. You don't need to. We'll talk about it later. For now we'll just call it a "C harp".

The Pocket Pal is a great beginner's instrument, and is the kind of harp almost everybody starts with. Once you get a little better, you can trade up. The back of the book has order forms for our free catalogue with more advanced harmonicas.

By way of introduction, blow and draw (suck) gently through the lower two or three holes of your harp and then slide up a couple of holes at a time, blowing and drawing all the way to the top.

Very occasionally, a defective reed gets by the people at Hohner, and if you're the lucky recipient of such an instrument, you can tell by a faint ringing sound in the affected hole. Or, alternatively, a reed won't play at all. Tap the harp on a soft surface, peer inside it, reason with it. Try to establish whose fault this is— yours or the instrument's.

Be aware, too, that a couple of notes, 2 draw and 3 draw especially, are tricky to play on any harp. So if your problem appears to be in either of these holes on the draw notes, hold off before you send it in. Wait until you've practiced your technique some.

If you do decide that you've gotten a lemon, return it to *Hohner Incorporated, Customer Services, Post Office Box 15033, Richmond, VA 23227.* Send along a cover note, and in most cases, they'll repair or replace at no charge.

The Cassette and the Book

This book is only half of a multi-media presentation. The other half is audio, and both are meant to be used side-by-side. They complement each other. On your cassette, you'll hear how the harmonica sounds when it's played correctly, and you'll also hear how it sounds when the notes are "cramped and hissy".

There are also whole sections of easy-to-play-with guitar music to give you a chance to play basic blues and country riffs. And you'll hear every riff and technique described in this book, including bent notes.

Although each can be used and understood independently, the book and cassette are programmed to go together. Read to page 18 in the book, and then turn on your cassette player and go through the first section. I'll take you by the hand at that point and lead you back and forth between the two as the need arises. To help you refer between the two, the tape is broken into sections and on most pages of the book, the corresponding tape section is notated like this: **1**

A Technical Note

Like every other cassette being manufactured these days, this tape is recorded at 1⅞ths of an inch per second. Exactly.

Unfortunately, among the millions of recorders floating around the country there is a significant degree of variation in the play-back speed. Some are a little fast. Some a little slow.

If your machine is really out of whack, it may make the notes sound a tad high or low.

The only real solution is to find another recorder, or better yet one with a variable speed control. But chances are, your machine is right on, and even if it's off by a fraction, if you're an easy going type of person, you won't be able to tell the difference.

CHAPTER
TWO

Straight
Harp

2

A Definition

There are two basic styles and feelings to harmonica music: "Straight Harp" and "Cross Harp".

"Cross Harp" we'll get to in Chapter V. "Straight Harp", the subject of this section, is most frequently played with simple melodies. It's the style most beginners start with. The accent is generally on the blow notes. Songs such as *Old Folks at Home, Streets of Laredo* and *You Are My Sunshine* are almost always played in the straight harp style, note for note, right on the melody.

What follow are a few melodies in the Straight Harp style. It's not too important to learn these tunes perfectly. You don't even have to blow or draw on single notes, just do it in the general area. The idea is to get acquainted with the instrument and its sound . . . and then move on. The section following this one describes the technique for getting single notes, the basic building block for both Straight and Cross Harp.

4 means blow on the 4 hole.   **④** means suck or draw on the 4 hole.

OH SUSANNAH

4 ④ 5　6　⑥6 5 4 ④ 5 ④ 4　④
Well I come from Alabama with my banjo on my knee

4 ④ 5 6　　⑥ 65 4 ④ 5　4 ④　4
And I'm going' to Louisiana oh my true love for to see.

⑤　　⑥　　⑥ 6　　　5 4 ④
Oh Susannah! Oh don't you cry for me.

4 ④　5　6　⑥6 5 4 ④ 5　4 ④　4
For I'm bound for Louisiana oh my true love for to see.

It's traditional to make *O Susannah* your first harmonica tune. Nobody knows why, everybody just does it.

Your First Sounds

Above all, a harmonica is not a tuba. You can't blast out good tone. It has to be coaxed, especially when you first start to play. As you blow and draw your way up and down the harmonica, be gentle yet firm.

- Make your breathing controlled and natural so your sound will be controlled and natural.

- Keep your lips moist to help the harmonica slide back and forth. Think of a typewriter carriage.

- Don't hold your lips down tightly on the harmonica.

- Try not to let saliva collect in the harp (yuck). Gently tapping the harp with the holes down on your palm or knee should take care of the problem.

- Be *gentle* as you blow and draw. Think nice thoughts.

- Keep the harmonica in its box when it's not in use. Little bits of dirt and whatnot can jam up the reeds.

- You may run across a harmonica expert who will tell you to soak your harp in water to improve its tone. Ignore him.

At this stage, you can play it in the "Close Enough Style". Just locate the general area on the harp and blow and draw appropriately. The idea is just to acquaint yourself with the sound of the instrument. Later on, when you've gotten your Single Note Pucker worked out, you can come back and put a little more finesse into it.

Incidentally, if you can't seem to find the right note to start on, just cover all the wrong holes with your index fingers, blow on the right one, memorize the sound, then take your fingers away and hunt around til you find it again.

YOU ARE MY SUNSHINE

3   4 ④ 5   ④5 4
You are my sunshine, my only sunshine,

4   ④ 5 ⑤ ⑥   6 ⑤   5
You make me happy when skies are grey

4   ④ 5 ⑤   ⑥   6 ⑤ 5 4
You'll never know dear, how much I love you,

4   ④ 5 ⑤ ④   5 4
Please don't take my sunshine away.

CLEMENTINE

4   3 5   4   5   6   ⑤ 5 ④
Oh my darlin', oh my darlin', oh my darlin', Clementine.

④ 5 ⑤   5 ④5 4   5 ④ 3 ③ ④ 4
You are lost and gone forever. Dreadful sorry, Clementine.

Appendix One contains an entire list of Straight Harp tunes (including that old favorite, the *Theme from the Lone Ranger*) but my sincere recommendation is that you start working on the next step, learning the Single Note, before you start expanding your repertoire.

CHAPTER

THREE

The Rich,
Clear
Single Note

3

Now that you've played around with some Straight Harp tunes in the Close-Enough Style, it's time to get a little more serious and focus on the Single Note.

This is the foundation of good harp playing. The unblurred, rich, clear, controlled single note. It's the most important skill you'll learn here, because it's the most beautiful voice your harmonica owns.

So what's the secret?

The Single Note Pucker *or* S.N.P.

Beginners always tend to be little shy with their harmonicas. Maybe you can relate to this: daintily you'll put the harp to your lips, as if you were about to plant a little peck on old Aunt Gertrude's cheek, and then you'll blow away.

The result is a hissy, multi-note effect.

This is *not* the path to harmonica satisfaction.

The best way to get a clear sweet single note is to push your lips out and place them well over the top and bottom plates of your harmonica. This is the key to the successful Single Note Pucker.

Try blowing on the 3 hole in this way. Are you getting the single note, or that blurred, chordy sound? Blow gently yet firmly, but don't puff your cheeks out. Your face should be relaxed, your lips soft, moist and puckered.

THE FURTHER YOU CAN PUT THE HARP IN YOUR MOUTH AND STILL GET ONE NOTE, THE BETTER WILL BE YOUR TONE. (This is Gindick's *Law of Unbridled Harmonica Passion*). Pressing your lips tightly on the harp won't work at all. The only pressure in your facial muscles should be in the corners of your lips and cheeks.

Work on both 3 blow and 4 draw. Your goal is to play without hiss, resistance or that blurred sound that comes from including notes to either side of the one you're aiming for.

Ten Minutes Later, and You Still Haven't Got It

Try thinking of your puckered lips as your instrument's mouthpiece, a tunnel that connects you to your harmonica. Streams of air are shaped and rounded in this mouthpiece by the way you mold it.

THE LARGER THE OPENING YOUR PUCKERED LIPS FORM, THE BETTER YOUR TONE WILL BE (Gindick's *Law of the Big Pucker*). The opening should be vertical. If it's wide and horizontal, you'll include side notes; if it's high and narrow, you'll get exactly the note you want, and you'll get all of it.

The muscle between your nostril and upper lip should be relaxed and almost perpendicular to your nose. Tightening this muscle, or curving it down onto the harp will cramp your tone up every time.

And NO CHEATING! Don't use your tongue to help find the hole you want, or curl it to guide the air. You're going to need that tongue as your percussion section later on, so keep it down and out of the way.

Practice, Practice, Practice

There's an old joke about a golf pro who had a standing promise to cut anyone's handicap in half with ten lessons for $25 apiece. Or, he said, he could do the same thing in a single lesson for $10,000. When someone objected to the price discrepancy, he told them, "If you want a miracle, you may as well pay for one."

The clear single note is the most important lesson in this book. And it won't come instantly. You've got to give it time. Take your practice sessions in short spurts, no marathons, you'll avoid the frustration syndrome that way. And use the straight harp tunes you've learned to practice on.

Speaking of practice, this is an area where the harmonica player is at a distinct advantage over, say, your average bassoonist. Because the harp is the ultimate portable instrument. Put it in your pocket and haul it out whenever you've got a moment or two—in the car especially. Anybody with a 45 minute commute is a potential harmonica virtuoso.

CHAPTER
FOUR
The Soul
of the
Harmonica

4

The harmonica is a uniquely emotional instrument. It's this quality that originally drew the bluesmen to the instrument, and it's this quality that can make a single note, or a single song, endlessly repeatable, and endlessly different.

For instance, the word "fire" can be stated flatly, posed as a question or hollered as a warning. Same word, but completely different meanings.

It's the same with the harmonica. You can give the notes you play any emotion you want simply by the *way* you play them.

Tonguing

Using your best Single Note Pucker, make a long single note sound on your 3 blow. Now, flick the tip of your tongue, as though you were saying *"ta ta ta"*, on the ridge just behind your upper teeth.

This *"ta ta ta"* tonguing action will stop and start the air traveling through the harmonica. And this will start and stop the sound. The result is total control of a crisp, rhythmic harp.

Vary the tempo and beat by making some sounds long and others short (*"taaaaaaa taaaaaaaa"* or *"ta ta taaaaaaa ta ta"*). Your tongue is your percussion section. No one-man band is complete without one.

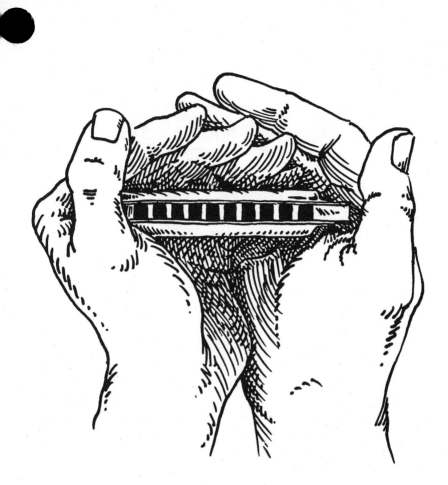

Hands

Your hands are wonderful tools for changing the sounds that come out of your harmonica. When they are closed, airtight, they mute the tone, and when they open, your harp says *"waaah"*. If you close and open several times, returning to a snug, airtight position each time, your harp says *"waaa waaa waaa"*.

With the help of your tape, experiment on your 3 blow and 4 draw. Remember, it's the movement of the hands from closed to open that makes your harp say *"waaaa"*, not just being in one position or another.

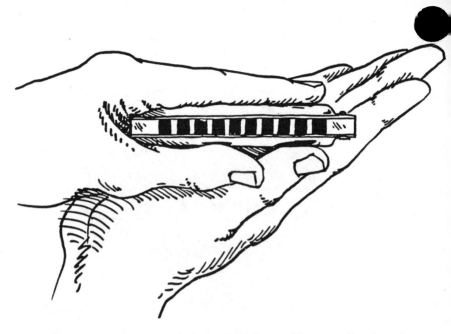

Fluttering one hand against the other with a gentle clapping motion will produce a warbling effect. Try this on holes 4 and 5 draw, and you'll get a sound like a train whistle.

As you play the Straight Harp songs from the first chapter, try using your hands to color the tone and produce feelings. Go from closed to open, and try the fluttering effect. Teach your harp to talk.

Putting It All Together: The Single Note Jam

Playing 3 blow and 4 draw alone might seem a little monotonous at first, but there is music to be made here. If you can't find it in these two notes, you won't find it anywhere.

Step 1: Get a beat going by stomping your foot 1-2-3-4, 1-2-3-4.

Step 2: Play long single notes on 3 blow.

Step 3: Use your tongue to punctuate your sound.

Step 4: Open and close your hands to add tone and color.

Step 5: And then slide to 4 draw and use the same techniques.

CHAPTER
FIVE
Cross Harp

5

So far we've been setting the foundation of your music: playing a few simple tunes, getting clean single notes, giving the notes emotion, and playing them with simple guitar music and solo.

Now we move into the heart and soul of the harmonica—*Cross Harp*. What follows is privileged information. It's the secret of getting a bluesy wailing sound on your instrument, and the secret of how to use that sound when accompanying guitarists, bands, records—even when you don't know the song they're playing, what you're doing, or what you're going to do next.

What It Is

"Cross Harp" is the sound of the blues. It accents the draw notes, and allows the player to wail, warble, create a sense of musical tension, "bend" or "choke" notes. Cross Harp is used mostly to play riffs, bluesy patterns of notes that accompany country western, blues and rock and roll. When people talk about the gritty soul of the harmonica, they're talking about Cross Harp.

Why Do They Call It "Cross Harp"?

Remember that C engraved on your harp that I told you to ignore at the beginning of the book?

Time to reconsider it.

Take up your C harp, make your mouth big and wide (forget the Single Note Pucker for now) and BLOW into holes 1, 2, 3, and 4.

On your C harp this is your C chord—a combination of notes merging to form one harmonious sound in the key of C. If you make these blow notes the basis of your music, you play Straight Harp in the key of C.

Now, instead of blowing on the four bottom holes of your C harp, DRAW. Welcome to a G chord. By accenting the individual notes of this draw chord, and a few other notes as well, you can play your C harmonica in the key of G. Hence the term "Cross Harp". (Read this paragraph again.)

That, in a nutshell, is the secret of blues harp. By playing a C harp with G key music, you're able to draw the key notes; and as I'll get into a little later, when you draw notes you can do things to them that you can't when you just blow them.

How Do I Do It?

By learning Gindick's nearly famous "Cross Harp System".

Chords are made up of Harmonizing Notes, notes that fit together and that fit in with the music played in their key. In the System, they're called "Safe Notes"—you can play them fearlessly and they won't make mistakes.

The Cross Harp System Safe Notes are the four draw notes on the bottom of your harp, 1 draw, 2 draw, 3 draw, and 4 draw. Plus, 3 blow, 6 blow and 6 draw.

When playing Cross Harp, these harmonizing Safe Notes establish the structure of your music.

Say you're accompanying a guitarist playing in the key of G. You can start in with a long, wailing 4 draw without fear of clashing, and then play up or down the harp to another Safe Note, maybe 3 blow or 6 draw—also Safe Notes.

Suddenly, you've got a dynamite harmonica riff.

But let's not get ahead of ourselves here. Listening to your cassette, experiment with the Harmonizing Notes by playing each with the guitar music. Prove to yourself that the Safe Notes fit in. You may not have the foggiest idea of how or why, but right now it doesn't matter. You're on your way to the blues.

Steppingstone Notes

Steppingstone Notes are not members of the Cross Harp Draw Chord. They do not automatically harmonize, and this is why you do not accent them.

Still, they're important.

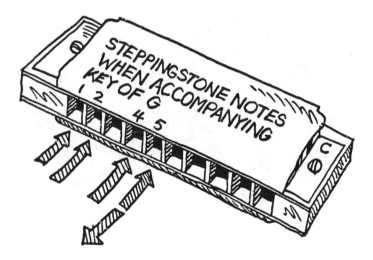

Steppingstone Notes serve as connectors between one harmonizing note and the next. Playing without Steppingstone Notes is like speaking without the words "and", "if" and "but".

The trick is to slide over them smoothly, with finesse. The Cross Harp Steppingstone Notes on the lower end of your harp are 1 blow, 2 blow, 4 blow, 5 draw and 5 blow. Play them lightly, on your tip toes.

If your harmonica clashes with the music on the tape, you've probably just accented one of these notes. The cassette will give you an idea of how it sounds when you play a Steppingstone too long, too loud, or at the wrong time.

Notes of Resolution and Wailing Notes

Now I want to go back and talk about Safe Notes again, since I left something out of the discussion earlier.

There are actually two kinds of Safe Notes: *Notes of Resolution* and *Wailing Notes*. Neither of these notes will make a mistake when played with the right key music, but they are very different sounding notes.

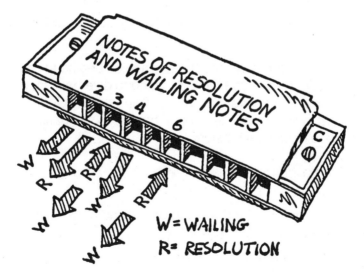

W = WAILING
R = RESOLUTION

To illustrate the way they differ, I want to use a metaphor:

The River of Music

Imagine music as a river, winding around curves, rolling downstream.

Now, add a harmonica to this river (remember, to play Cross Harp in the key of G, use your C harp). The harmonica begins in the river, rises smoothly from the water, finds a good strong note, holds it for several beats, tonguing, bending, creating a good strong feeling of musical tension.

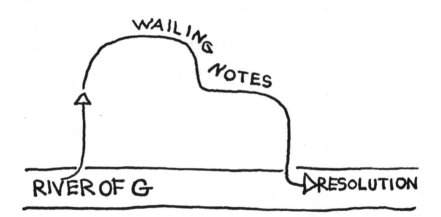

Then there's a pause, and the harmonica begins to return to the water. Just when you think it's going to dive back in, it finds another note just above the water to hang on for a long sleepy moan that creates more tension. Finally, it eases back into the river and releases the tension.

When the harmonica is in the river, it's playing a *Note of Resolution.*

When it's bending and twisting on one note that's out of the water, it's playing a *Wailing Note.*

The notes in between are *Steppingstone Notes.*

Any kind of cohesive storytelling, and this includes blues and country harp music, attempts to build tension and release it. Wailing Notes and Notes of Resolution are *both* Safe Notes, but Wailing Notes create tension and Notes of Resolution resolve it. One of the secrets of playing Cross Harp is building tension on your Wailing Notes and resolving it on the Notes of Resolution, while moving smoothly between the two on the Steppingstones.

But enough theory. Time to put all this to work.

WAILING

RESOLUTION

Your Very First Riff

You're about to learn what is probably the most important riff in this book: The Up and Down Blues Riff. You should learn it so that you can play it in your sleep. You can do it a million different ways, in a million different songs.

The Up and Down Blues Riff

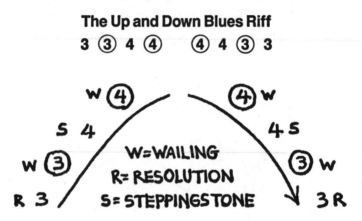

A reminder: By this time, you should be hitting single notes cleanly, (at least some of the time). If you still get that blurred multi-note effect all of the time, go back to the Single Note Pucker section and work on that a bit more.

As you work on this riff, try to make the changes between 3 and 4 as smooth as you can (lick your lips and move your harp, not your head). And when you reverse the direction of your breath from blow to draw, try to do it cleanly, evenly.

The 4 blow is a Steppingstone, so play it lightly, then wail on the 4 draw. Use your tongue and hands to color it and create tension. Then pause, and start back down to the river. Wail on the 4 draw, blow on the 4, slide over to the 3 and draw on it with a bit of funk to create tension. And then finally land on your Note of Resolution, the 3 blow.

Then do it all over again. Differently.

The Up and Down Riff: Take 2

Four draw is one of your most important Wailing Notes. Create tension on it by playing the "up" part of this riff three times in a row before finally landing hard on the 3 blow Note of Resolution.

This is like asking a question three times and not getting an answer. It makes the listener yearn for that story ender, 3 blow.

$$3 \enspace ③ \enspace 4 \enspace ④ \enspace ..?$$
$$3 \enspace ③ \enspace 4 \enspace ④ \enspace ..?$$
$$3 \enspace ③ \enspace 4 \enspace ④ \enspace ..?$$
$$④ \enspace 4 \enspace ③ \enspace ..3!$$

Same Riff: Take 3

Play the "down" part of this riff twice, building an expectation for a third time. Then, turn it around by playing the 4 Draw Surprise, building even more tension. Finally, resolve it all with a final Down Riff, hitting the 3 blow Note of Resolution.

$$④ \enspace 4 \enspace ③ \enspace 3$$
$$④ \enspace 4 \enspace ③ \enspace 3$$
$$④ \enspace 4 \enspace ③ \enspace .④!? \quad (the \; Surprise)$$
$$④ \enspace 4 \enspace ③ \enspace 3$$

Adding Rhythm

For those of you learning without the benefit of the tape, you'll have to set up your own beat since you won't have the recorded guitar to listen to.

But it's not that hard. You can find rhythm almost anywhere. Probably the easiest is to stomp your foot in a regular pattern (*one-two-three-four* and *one-two-three-four* ... and watch out for downstairs neighbors).

Or you can play along with the clank of a washing machine, your footsteps as you walk along, the dripping of a faucet, the regular sound of your rear wheel bearings going out ... it doesn't really matter where you get it, but the underlying beat you put to your music is essential. Without it, your riffs will wander around without form or focus.

For Tape Listeners

The guitar music on your tape is in the key of G, the Cross Harp key of your C harmonica, so you can jam along without fear of clashing.

Keep in mind though:

• Start slowly. Oftentimes the best way to enter a song is with a long 3 blow or 4 draw, instead of playing lots of notes very quickly.

• Use your best Single Note Pucker for the cleanest notes.

• Color your music, and give it a beat, with your hands and tongue.

• If you make a mistake (sound a clashing note), you've probably just accented a Steppingstone (4 blow?). DO NOT stop playing. Just continue on your way to a Note of Resolution or a Wailing Note.

• When in doubt, fake it.

CHAPTER
SIX

**Expanding
Your Keyboard—
Cross Harp on
Holes 1–6**

6

By this time you ought to be fairly smooth moving between holes 3 and 4, whether blowing or drawing. You ought to have worked over the Up and Down Riff and its variations until you can play them backwards and forwards. And in the process of jamming along with the tape, you should have dreamed up a few wrinkles of your own.

And, of course, if you're really making progress, you should have made a couple of thousand of mistakes by now.

If you've done all this, it's time to widen your horizons.

Holes 1 through 6 are the meat and potatos of blues and country harmonica. These are the notes that have the deep, throaty sound. These are the notes you can bend and twist. And, thank goodness, these are the notes that are easiest to play.

There are three Notes of Resolution between holes 1 and 6: 2 draw, 3 blow and 6 blow. (By the way, in case you haven't noticed by now, 2 draw and 3 blow are the same note).

Each gives you plenty of opportunity for creating networks of riffs that start on one Note of Resolution, create tension on the Wailing Notes and end on another Note of Resolution.

But don't get carried away with all the new options. In most cases, the best harmonica music is simple music—well played. This is Gindick's *Principal of Repetition and Don't Get Too Fancy.* Far better to play one note with good feeling, timing and tone, than to play complicated riffs that go from one end of the harp to the other, if they're poorly timed or out of place.

Enough lecturing. We'll start with a map of the Cross Harp System. Then we'll focus on 6 draw and blow. The feeling is a bit different on these new holes, so you'll have to approach them with an open mind and a quality Single Note Pucker.

MAP OF CROSS HARP SYSTEM
HOLES 1-6

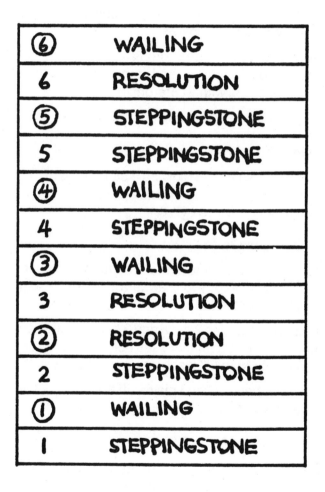

⑥	WAILING
6	RESOLUTION
⑤	STEPPINGSTONE
5	STEPPINGSTONE
④	WAILING
4	STEPPINGSTONE
③	WAILING
3	RESOLUTION
②	RESOLUTION
2	STEPPINGSTONE
①	WAILING
1	STEPPINGSTONE

A Riff for the *Really* Hopeless: The 6 Draw Solo

The 6 hole of your harp is a particularly versatile one; it contains both a Wailing Note and a Note of Resolution. This happy fact suggests the world's simplest riff, the 6 Wail and Blow.

Without ever leaving the 6 hole you can create a riff that will almost always fit right in. How?

Wail on that 6 draw, flutter it, break it up with your tongue, create all the tension you can . . . and then resolve it with the 6 blow. And then back again, with a different feel.

Try it, you'll be amazed at how well this works.

The Down and Out Riff

You can also use your 6 blow as a starting point for a riff that takes you down to the wailer 4 draw, and then finally lands on the resolution 3 blow: 6 ⑤ ④ 3.

Now For Your Low Notes

Holes 1 and 2 have some of the best notes on your harp. One draw is a Wailing Note; two draw is a Note of Resolution; two blow is a Steppingstone.

As I mentioned earlier, 2 draw and 3 blow are the same notes. But when I'm playing a riff that uses holes 3 and 4, I usually use the 3 blow as my Note of Resolution.

On the other hand, when I play a riff that uses holes 1 and 2, I use 2 draw as my Note of Resolution.

The Black Holes of 2 and 3 Draw

Before I get started on the riffs located down in these two holes, I want to describe a problem that affects a lot of beginners, known as the *"What the !#%&'s Wrong With This 2 Hole?"* problem.

If you haven't already, try drawing on your 2 hole, and then your 3 draw. Are they hard to play? Resistant? Can you get anything to come out of them at all?

If the answer is "no", cheer up. This is a common problem. And to answer your question, it's not your harp. It's you.

Sorry about that.

Two draw and 3 draw are two of the most difficult notes on your harp. Four draw and 6 draw are much easier. They'll let you get away with drawing too hard, with your upper lip pressed down, your pucker too small, your jaw clenched. You can make all the mistakes, 4 draw and 6 draw will let it ride (although they may sound a little flat).

Two draw won't put up with this nonsense. This is a note that really tests your single note playing ability. IF YOU DON'T PLAY IT RIGHT, IT WON'T PLAY. Three draw is very much the same way.

If you've got this problem, and most beginners do, here's a list of time-tested helpful hints:

- Start with a completely empty set of lungs and slowly fill them up through the 2 draw. Even if the note doesn't appear at the beginning of this 30 second inhale, concentrate on keeping it even and steady, and it may well show up towards the end.

- Relax your mouth and face. You'll never be able to force these notes out. They have to be coaxed.

- As you're playing, think about your upper lip. Is it clamped down hard on the harp, like I've been nagging you not to? Move the instrument up towards your nose. This should push your lips up and allow your upper lip to be CURVED UP and OUT as described in the Single Note Pucker section.

- *Important.* Draw the airstream up to the roof of your mouth. Feel the air tickling your nostrils. This feeling of drawing the air UP is called "playing from your head". It's a key to getting these notes to sound right.

An important side-benefit to perfecting the 2 and 3 draw is the effect it'll have on all your notes. If your technique is good enough to get the hard notes, the easy ones will sound fuller and stronger.

The Good Morning Riff

Having been warned about the problem, you're ready to take on what may be my all-time favorite musical phrase, The Good Morning Riff, just about the most versatile riff in the book. You can play it with blues, country western or rock. You can play it slow, fast or in-between, it always seems to fit right in.

① 2 ②

The 2 draw Note of Resolution is the note you want to emphasize. Both the 1 draw and 2 blow should be played quickly and smoothly. Once you get to the 2 draw, hold it a little bit longer. You may want to tongue it to give it some feeling and to help it fit in with the music.

There's a little blues song you can play by alternating different versions of The Good Morning Riff: first, tongue the 2 draw twice, then, next time around, don't tongue it at all. It'll sound like two entirely different riffs.

CHAPTER
SEVEN

Bending...
or More Magic
on the Harmonica

Before jumping into this, let's review where you are: You've got a great (or at least near-great) Single Note Pucker. You can play pure clean single notes on holes 1 through 6. You've learned the basic variations of The Up and Down Riffs and Good Morning Riffs and you've even made up a few of your own.

You think you're ready for the Big Time, bending notes.

What It Is

Bending is the sound of a clear single note, say 4 draw, slurring down so that it sounds almost like a 4 blow, and then coming back up.

If you could see a picture of it, this is what it would look like.

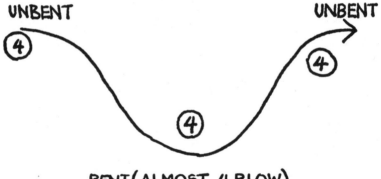

On holes 1 through 6, you can only bend the draw notes— perfect for Cross Harp, because it's the draw notes that create tension. And bending is a technique that goes hand in hand with tension building.

Step one in learning how to bend notes is establishing clear, clean single notes—and the test for this is your 2 draw. If you can pull a pure note out of this trouble-maker, then you're probably about ready.

Doing It

Start with a good, clear single note on 4 draw. Use your best pucker and be sure your harp is deep in your lips.

Now, pull the airstream down into your throat, feel some pressure in there. (When you're bending, you're going to be "playing from the body" rather than "from the head.")

And then, release the airstream from the bottom of your throat so that it goes back to hitting the roof of your mouth. If everything is working right, the note should bend down almost to where it sounds like 4 blow, and then snap back up when you release.

Look at the diagram for an illustration of what I mean by this.

STRAIGHT NOTE   BENT NOTE

By now you've probably tried this little trick a couple of times. And what happened? Let me guess . . .

You started with a medium clear 4 draw, and then, just like it says here in the book, you began re-directing your airstream lower, towards the back of your throat and down. Gradually you began to swell up—balloon-fish style. Your eyes began bugging out. A harsh gargling sound began emerging from somewhere near the base of your esophagus (how'm I doing?). . .

Meanwhile, that 4 draw has started to fade out for want of air, and besides, it's hard to hear over the gargle. But did it ever even drop a fraction of a note?

Of course not. And that illustration made it seem so simple.

So now what? You've tried wiggling your tongue, grimacing your mouth, crossing your eyes . . . and still no bent notes.

The Whistling Analogy

Think about the way you whistle for a moment. When you whistle, you change the shape of your mouth to change the tone of the notes. It's the same with bending.

Try this for a second. Whistle the highest note you can reach, and then lower it all the way down. Think about how the direction of the airstream changed. (If you can whistle on the inhale, this is easy. If you can't, just think in reverse.) On the high notes, the airstream hits the roof of your mouth; on the lower notes, the back of your throat.

Now if that made any sense, apply it to your harmonica.

Didn't make any sense? OK, let's try another one.

The *Weeeee/Euuuuuu* Approach

Take the harp away from your mouth and DRAWWWW through your puckered lips. Listen to the hiss of air. By changing the shape of your lips, make that hiss sound like *Weeeee.*

Now, hollow out your mouth and arch your tongue back into your throat. The hiss should sound like *Euuuuu.* Do this several times in a row on the same breath of air, *Weeeee Euuuuuu Weeee* (Are we having fun yet?).

After you've recovered from this, try doing it on your 4 draw. Establish a good clear note *(Weeeee),* and then begin pulling it down *(Euuuuuu),* finally letting it back up *(Weeeee).*

Some Hints

Different people have different problems with bending. What follows is a list of all the helpful hints I've ever used in teaching. Try them all in turn and see if one doesn't key right into your particular problem.

- Start with a good, clean, single note. Push your lips out.
- Be certain your pucker is as big and oval shaped as you can make it without including side notes.
- Put your harp into your mouth just a little further than seems reasonable.
- No wiggling of the tongue or grimacing of the face.
- Do NOT draw harder when it doesn't work.
- DO pull a full, steady airstream down to the bottom of the back of your throat.
- DO arch the back of your tongue.
- DO hollow out your mouth and throat.
- DO feel a sense of air pressure down in your throat as you attempt to bend your 4 draw; and DO release that pressure from your throat as you bring the note back up.
- Do NOT give up. Try it in little bite-sized sessions. No tear-stained marathons. You'll eventually get it, and when you do, you'll wonder what the problem was in the first place.

Now That You've Got It

How long it will take you to start bending notes reliably depends on a number of things, not the least of which is how much time you've got to practice, but once it starts happening, here are some of the places you can take it:

The Wailing Bend

Making the 4 draw go up and down very quickly is called the Wailing Bend. Try it at the top of the Up Riff.

3 ③ 4 ④

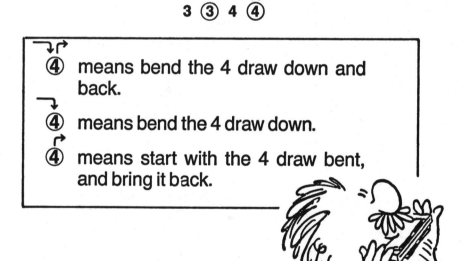

④ means bend the 4 draw down and back.

④ means bend the 4 draw down.

④ means start with the 4 draw bent, and bring it back.

The 2 Step Bend

Start on the 4 draw playing it bent. Then bring it back up. Try the 2 Step on the 4 draw at the top of the Up Riff.

3 3 4 ④

And try incorporating both these bends into The Good Morning Riff, The Down and Out Riff as well as the 6 Draw Solo.

Good Morning ① 2 ② *or* ① 2 ②

Down and Out 6 ⑤ ④ 3 *or* 6 ⑤ ④ 3

6 Draw Solo 6 ⑥ 6 *or* 6 ⑥ 6

The Amazing Three Draw Bend

When playing folk, country or mellow rock, you usually don't bend the 3 draw note, but when the subject is blues, it's the note you want to stress. Three draw bent may be the bluest note in your harp.

Despite the fact that I've been calling 3 draw a Wailing Note, it doesn't *really* create any tension until you bend it.

And the amazing thing about 3 draw is that you can bend it down not just one step, but two: bent and super-bent.

To bend your 3 draw into these lower regions, you need to open up your throat and pull the note way down. When I say "Open your throat," I mean exactly that. Pull the air down, down, down—so that you can feel it in the place you yawn from.

In terms of the *Weeeee/Euuuuu* theory, this means your drawn airstream should do a Super *Euuuuu*. This may take a little force, but don't overdo it.

Your tone may sound a little hoarse or raspy at first but that's OK. As a matter of fact, the distorted 3 draw is a characteristic sound of blues and country harmonica. It can put real grit into your playing.

Use your hands to mellow out your tone and to give you better control over the airstream and the bend.

The 3 Draw Slide

Start the note in its unbent position and bring it down: then play your 3 blow.

③ 3

Then, turn it around and let the note slide back up.

③ 3

In the Down Riff, use this bend to really create tension:

④ 4 ③ 3

Stress the 3 draw wailer; pull it way down and gently resolve on the 3 blow.

Three Bent and 3 Blow Boogie

Another one hole jam that'll get them up and stomping around.

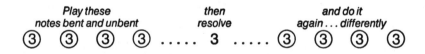

Play these
notes bent and unbent   *then*   *and do it*
         resolve   *again . . . differently*
③ ③ ③ ③ . . . . . 3 . . . . . ③ ③ ③ ③

The 2 Draw Bend

As I mentioned before, 2 draw and 3 blow are one and the same notes: 3 blow is easier to play, but 2 draw you can bend.

It's quite possible that if your unbent 2 draws are low, distorted and a bit out of tune, that you're already bending 2 draw by accident. Congratulations.

Now the trick is to learn how to play it unbent, with the air-stream coming through free and easy. And then to be able to switch back, by pulling the air deep into your open throat.

Practice all this on the Up Down Up Bend: ②

Hint: Be sure you're getting a good unbent single note before you start your bend. And start with your hands open, close them as you draw the note down, release them as you bring the note all the way up to its unbent position again.

For additional practice, work on a two step bend (starting in the bent position, and then releasing up) and use it in the Good Morning Riff:

① 2 ②

EIGHT

Taking Your Act on the Road

You're becoming a harp player.

You play in your car, you play when going for a walk, and they're even starting to let you play around the house. Sometimes, when you've just played an unexpectedly nice riff, you've even thought about playing with other people—jamming.

Doing it, is what this chapter is about.

Getting together with other people in a musical jam may well be one of life's finest hours. Using homemade music to communicate with you won't believe how fast you can turn a group of strangers into a bunch of friends.

Although it may seem hard to believe, if you've made it this far ... you've learned enough to have this experience ... even enjoy it. Your instrument played in the Cross Harp style is made for accompaniment. You can plug the riffs you already know in and out of zillions of songs and they'll instantly sound better, with more soul and "feel". Plus, you'll be having one of life's few Truly Great Times. Trust me.

WANTED: One Guitarist

The harmonica and guitar are a musical match, they have complementary sounds, and your first step should be finding someone to play with. Keep your eyes open for stray guitar players, friends you know who occasionally plunk around, or maybe friends of friends. Put up a notice at the local music store, the world is full of guitarists, but us dynamite harp players are in short supply.

It might even be a spur of the moment thing, out on some lawn somewhere with a complete stranger. Don't be shy, step right up, pull out your harp, raise an eyebrow and ask him or her the world's only guaranteed opening line:

What Key Are You In?

Songs can be played in virtually any of the 12 possible musical keys, but oftentimes a guitarist or group will know a tune in only one or two. As a result, it makes sense to start building up a quiver of different key harps if you plan to play with people very much.

If you add a G, D, F and maybe an A to your C harp, you'll be able to play along with 90% of the music you run across. If you haven't tried a different key harp before, you'll discover that all the old riffs still work, they'll just be pitched higher or lower. (The back of the book has an order form).

So let's say your new partner tells you the song is in the key of C, what harp do you pull out?

It depends. If you want to play Straight Harp, and help pick out the melody line, get your C harp out. But unless I were a real natural, or knew the tune, I'd be a little hesitant about trying it in the Straight Harp style. At first at least, I'd try to accompany by playing Cross Harp, just like you've done with your practice tape.

And which harp plays "Cross" with the key of C? In order to find out, you need to be able to: (1) Count to 4 and (2) Know the first 7 letters of the alphabet, A B C D E F G.

In our example, begin with the letter C since that's the key we're working from. Then count up the alphabet 4 letters (I use my fingers), "C D E *F*". And pull out your F harp.

If your guitarist is playing something in the key of E (a common blues key), count "E F G" and then, since you've run out of letters, go back to "A". And pull out your A harp.

If you forget this "Count to Four" rule, or if you run across an oddball tune being played in a sharp or flat key, what follows is a chart with all the answers:

If the guitar is playing a tune in the key of . . .	Pull out a harp in the key of . . .
A	D
B flat	E flat
B	E
C	F
D flat	F sharp
D	G
E flat	A flat
E	A
F	B flat
F sharp	B
G	C

Tuning Up

Before you can play along though, the guitar must be tuned to your harmonica. If you're going to sit in with a band, hopefully they're already in tune and you can skip this step, but with an individual guitarist you should let him or her tune to you.

Probably the easiest way to do this is to simply blow on the first hole of your harp. The note you create will be the same as the note engraved on the top of your harp. If you have an E harp, use this one as your "tune-to" harp, even if you won't be using it in the song. The guitar has two E strings and it's an easy note to work from.

On a C harp, you can either blow on the first hole and let your guitarist tune to your C note, or you can blow in the 2 or 5 holes. Either of these creates an E note and your guitarist can tune to that.

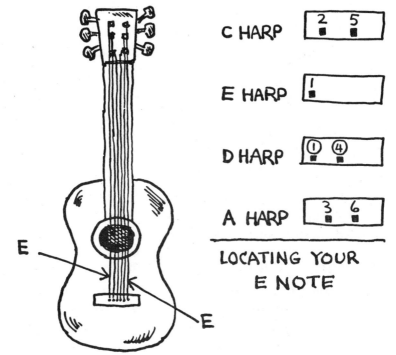

C HARP ⏣ 2 5

E HARP ⏣ 1

D HARP ⏣ ① ④

A HARP ⏣ 3 6

LOCATING YOUR
E NOTE

Starting In

You've got your right key harp, your guitarist is tuned to you, you're all set to go . . . So what's your first move?

Nothing. Just listen. Get a feel for the chord progression and rhythm. It's just like your practice tape. When you can anticipate the chord changes, start in with one of your Safe Notes. In the C harp, more than likely this will be 3 blow or 4 draw. Hold it for a couple of beats and play it softly. Maybe you can add some feeling by tonguing or using your hands.

If your single note is fitting, and nobody seems to be complaining yet, try one of your basic riffs. Play it quietly; you're still just experimenting. Repeat it a few times. Remember Gindick's *Principle of Repetition and Don't Get Too Fancy.* Your goal isn't to sound like a star just yet. It's to help the other guy sound good.

After you've set up a musical "hook" or theme by playing one riff over and over, expand on it. Maybe a move up to 6 blow or 6 draw. Maybe a long 3 draw bent or link some of your riffs together.

For instance, play the Good Morning Riff so it takes you up to 3 draw: (1) 2 (2)(3) .
Or continue up to the 4 draw: (1) 2 (2)(3) 4 (4) .

From either the 3 or 4 draw, you can use the Down Riff, (4) 4 (3) 3, to get yourself back to resolution. Or you can slide the harp from 4 draw up to 6 draw and wail on that note before resolving on the 6 blow, (4) . . . (6) 6.

And if you make a mistake by accenting a clashing note or something, don't worry about it. Just grin your way right through it and get back to a Safe Note. Then start in again.

Listening to the Guitar's Chord Patterns

Guitar chords (like most all music) follows the familiar tension and resolution pattern that I've talked about so much. Chords, incidentally, are just patterns of notes that harmonize together, and they are named just like notes or keys, A B C etc. The appendix on musical theory will give you the details but the basic idea is very frequently the same as you're already familiar with: Chords of Resolution, and chords that lead away from them . . . and back to them.

The Chord of Resolution is usually the place where the verse begins and also where it comes to an end. For instance, if the song goes . . .

"This land is your land,
this land is my land,
from California
to the New York island."

The word "This" and the word "island" will both fall on the guitar's Chord of Resolution. A lot of songs are structured this way.

As an accompanying harp player, you should try to anticipate the point where the chord progression returns to the Chord of Resolution and resolve your harmonica patterns at the same time.

Don't worry if this doesn't feel naturally easy. It isn't. It takes time and experience. The more you jam with records, tapes and other instruments, the better you'll get.

Playing With Singers

As a harp player, you should not play continuously. Far better to phrase your riffs, weave them in and out. Play your "hook", let 4 beats pass, and then play it again.

This is especially true when you're playing with singers. Don't play over them. A better idea is to echo the lyrics with simple *wah wah's*. Don't forget, you're a supporting character in this act—usually.

Taking a Lead

But then comes that terrifying moment when the singer stops, and the guitar player nods at you signifying that it's your turn to take a lead.

In most cases, the guitar music will continue playing the same chord progression as before. Your job is to play loudly and confidently and—usually—simply. Even if you haven't any idea what they're doing, at least fake it with pride. Don't try to play the same notes as the vocalist was singing. Take your usual riffs and put all the feeling you can into them.

Through your lead, you can either play continuously, linking one riff to the next, or else phrase your riffs with pauses in between.

Typically, the guitar will go through its chord progression twice. It's a good idea to count on that and keep your playing simpler the first time through. The second time around, if you can, use riffs a little more complicated and build to the end. Great dramatic technique.

What If They're Playing Something Besides Country and Blues?

Assuming you're not trying to sit in with the Philadelphia Philharmonic or a modern jazz quintet, you should have no problem. Traditional folk music, dance tunes, rock & roll, reggae . . . you can accompany them all. They all utilize the same basic musical structure. The main difference is in the rhythm and feeling.

A singer is in exactly the same situation. There are only 12 notes on the scale. It doesn't matter if the music is country or rock, the singer needs to give the notes a feeling that matches the music, just like you'll have to.

A Little More on the Straight Harp vs. Cross Harp Question

I want to say a few more words on this since it's a question that is answered best by experience—there are no good hard and fast rules. Particularly as you become more accomplished, you'll be able to do more in both styles and each tune will have to be approached with an open mind and two harps at hand.

Still, there are a couple of helpful tips:

Straight harp is champion at playing melodies. For instance, if you're going to accompany a group of swaying Rotarians at a New Years Eve party in a stirring rendition of *Auld Lang Syne*, you probably want to play Straight Harp. This is a straightforward song and the straight style gives it the right treatment.

On the other hand, if the accompaniment is playing Willie Nelson, or some Rolling Stones . . . or even some Bing Crosby, you should probably play Cross Harp. It has a more soulful, gritty feel. And, in the style of rock, country or blues, it's better for creating tension.

To sum things up: For blues, you always play Cross Harp. For rock and country, you ALMOST always play Cross Harp. For folk, it's about half and half; and for melodies, it's usually straight.

Personally, when I'm learning a new song, I usually try it both ways and see which sounds best.

CHAPTER
NINE
Where To From Here

9

You can spend a contented, deeply fulfilled lifetime playing harmonica solo. I have a harp that I keep around the office for doodling with on breaks. I have a couple in my car that I must have logged a couple of hundred thousand miles on. And when I'm sitting down somewhere, or out for a walk, I can usually stick my hand in my pocket and expect to come out with an old E harp.

But I've also sat in with everything from punk bands to church choirs, joined in with sidewalk folk singers, midnight blues guitarists and teenage rock and roll bands—and those are the times that I really remember.

If you've come this far, you've probably already discovered the secret that's kept me tootling on this instrument for fifteen years, and, more than likely, kept you plugging away to the end of this book.

It's simple: Music is a higher form of communication. It says better things in better ways.

So pull out that harp and spread the word.

APPENDIX
ONE
A Mostly Straight Harp Repertoire

THEME FROM THE LONE RANGER (straight harp)

3   4   (4)   5
dada dum dada dum dada dum dum dum

3   4   5 (4)   (3)   3
dada dum dada dum dada dum dum

3   4   (4)   5
dada dum dada dum dada dum dum dum

4 5   6   5 (4) 4   5   4
dada dummm . . . dada dum dum dum
Heigh ho Silver, away!

STREETS OF LAREDO (straight harp)

3   4   (4)   5   (4) 4 (3) 3
As I walked out in the streets of Laredo,

3   4   (4)   5 (4) 4   (4)
As I walked out in Laredo one day,

6   (5) 5   (5)   5 (4) 5   (4) 4   (3) 3
I spied a young cowboy all wrapped in white linen,

3   4   (4) 5 (4) 5 (5)   5   4 (4) 4
All wrapped in white linen, and as cold as the clay.

STREETS OF LAREDO (cross harp)

(1) (2)   (3)′   (3)   (3)′ 3 (2) (1)
As I walked out in the streets of Laredo,

(1) (2)   (3)′   (3) (3)′ 3   (3)′
As I walked out in Laredo one day,

(4)   4 (3)   4 (3) (3)′ (3)   (3)′ 3 (2)′ (1)
I spied a young cowboy all wrapped in white linen,

(1) (2)   (3)′ (3) (3)′ (3) 4   (3) (2) (3)′ 3
All wrapped in white linen and as cold as the clay.

◯′means play the note only in its bent position.

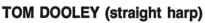

TOM DOOLEY (straight harp)

6   ⑥   7   8
Hang down your head Tom Dooley
6   ⑥   7   8
Hang down your head and cry
6   ⑥   7   ⑧
Hang down your head Tom Dooley,
⑧   7   ⑥   7
Poor boy, you're bound to cry.

TOM DOOLEY (cross harp)

①   2   ② ③
Hang down your head Tom Dooley
①   2   ② ③╱
Hang down your head and cry
①   2   ② ③╱
Hang down your head Tom Dooley,
③╱   3   2   3
Poor boy, you're bound to cry.

SHE'LL BE COMIN' ROUND THE MOUNTAIN (straight harp)

6   ⑥ 7   ⑥   6   5   6   7
She'll be coming round the mountain when she comes,
7   ⑧ 8   9   8   ⑧   7   ⑧
She'll be coming round the mountain when she comes,
9   ⑨ 8   ⑧   7
She'll be coming round the mountain
7   ⑥   ⑧   7
She'll be coming round the mountain
6   8   ⑧   7   ⑦   7
She'll be coming round the mountain when she comes.

SHE'LL BE COMING ROUND THE MOUNTAIN (cross harp)

①　2 ②　　　　　2 ①　　　　2 ②
She'll be coming round the mountain when she comes,

2　③③　　　　④ ③　③′ 3 ③′
She'll be coming round the mountain when she comes,

④　4 ③　　　　③′ 3
She'll be coming round the mountain,

3　　2　　　　③′ 3
She'll be coming round the mountain,

①　　　　　　③ ③′ ③ ②②
She'll be coming round the mountain when she comes.

CAMPTOWN RACES (straight harp)

6　　　　5 6 ⑥　6 5　　5 ④　5 ④
Camptown ladies sing this song, dooh dah, dooh dah;

6　　　　5 6　⑥ 6　　5 ④ 5　④ 4
Camptown racetrack five miles long, oh dooh dah day.

4　　　5 6 7　⑥　7 ⑥ 6
Gonna run all night; gonna run all day.

6　　　5　6　⑥ 6 5　④　5 ⑤ 5 ④ 4
Bet my money on the bobtail nag; somebody bet on the bay.

WILDWOOD FLOWER (straight harp)

5 ⑤ 6　⑥ 7 5 ⑤ 5 ④ 5 ④　4
I will twine and will mingle my raven black hair

5　⑤ 6 ⑥7 5 ⑤ 5 ④5 ④4
With the roses so red and the lily so fair.

6 7 8 ⑧ 7 6⑥ 7　⑥　6
The myrtle so green of a bright emerald hue,

4④ 5 6⑥65 4 ④　5 ④ 4
The pale emanita, and eyes look so blue.

74

YOU ARE MY SUNSHINE (straight harp)

3 4 ④ 5   5 ④5 4
You are my sunshine, my only sunshine
4 ④ 5 ⑤⑥ ⑥ 6 ⑤ 5
You make me happy, when skies are grey,
4 ④5 ⑤ ⑥ ⑥ 6 ⑤ 5 4
You never know dear, how much I love you,
4   ④ 5 ⑤ ④   5 4
Please don't take my sunshine away.

SWING LOW, SWEET CHARIOT (cross harp)

③   3   ③ 3 2① 3   ③④ 5 ④
Swing low, sweet chariot, coming for to carry me home.
5 ④③   ④ 3 2① 3   ③3 2 3
Swing low, sweet chariot, coming for to carry me home.

SHENANDOAH (straight harp)

3   4   ④5 ⑤⑥ 6 7⑦⑥6 ⑥ 6 5 6
Oh Shenandoah, I love to wander. Away, you rolling river.
5 6 ⑥   5 6 5 ④ 4 4 ④ 5 4 5 ⑥6
Oh Shenandoah, I love to wander. Look away, oh look away.
4   ④ 5 4 ④ 4
Cross the wide Missouri.

OL' STEWBALL (straight harp)

3 4   ④ 5   ④ 4   3 4 ④ 5 ④
Ol' Stewball was a racehorse, an I wish he were mine.
④ 5 ⑤ 5④③ 4   ④ 4
He never drank water; he always drank wine.

CLEMENTINE (straight harp)

4   3 5   4 4 5 6   ⑤ 5 ④
Oh my darlin', oh my darlin', oh my darlin', Clementine.

④ 5 ⑤   5 ④ 5 4   4 5 ④ 3 ③ ④ 4
You are lost and gone forever, dreadful sorry, Clementine.

WASHBASH CANNONBALL (straight harp)

6   7   8
I stood on the Atlantic Ocean

8   ⑧ 7 ⑥
On the wide Pacific shore

6   ⑦   ⑧
Heard the Queen of the mountains

⑦   ⑥   6
To the South Bay by the door.

6   7   8
She's long, she's tall and handsome.

8   ⑧ 7 ⑥
She's loved by one and all,

⑥   6   ⑦   ⑧
She's the modern combination,

⑦   6 ⑥ ⑦ 8
Called the Wabash Cannonball.

AMAZING GRACE (straight harp)

3 4 5   5   ④ 4   3
Amazing grace, how sweet the sound,

3   4 5 5   ④ 6
That saved a wretch like me.

6 ⑥ 6 5 ④ 4   3
I once was lost but now am found,

3   4 5   ④ 4
Was blind but now I see.

OLD FOLKS AT HOME (straight harp)

5   ④ 4 5 ④ 4 7 ⑥ 7
Way down upon the Swanee River

6   5 4 ④
Far, far away.

5   ④ 4 5 ④ 4 7 ⑥7
That's where my heart is turning over,

6   5 4 ④   4
That's where the old folks stay.

FRANKIE AND JOHNNY (straight harp)

4 ④ 5 ⑥ 6 ⑥ 4
Frankie and Johnny were lovers

4 ④ 5 ⑥ 6 ⑥ 4
Oh Lordy how they could love

7   ⑥ 6 7   ⑥   6
They swore to be true to each other

7   ⑦⑥ 6
True as the stars above

5 6 ⑥ ④ 6   ⑥ 6 5 4
He was her man, but he was doing her wrong.

RED RIVER VALLEY (straight harp)

3 4 5   ④ 5 ④ 4
From this valley they say you are going,

3 4 5 4 5 6 ⑤ 5 ④
We will miss your bright eyes and sweet smile,

6 ⑤ 5   ④ 4 ④ 5 6 ⑤
For they say you are taking the sunshine,

3 3   ③ 4 ④ 5 ④ 4
That has brightened our pathways awhile.

BANKS OF THE OHIO (straight harp)

4   5 4   5 ④
I asked my love to take a walk,

④   5 ⑤   6 ⑥6 5
Just a little walk, just a little walk,

 5   6   ⑥ 6   ⑤
Down beside where the waters flow,

 4   ④   5   3   5④ 4
Down by the banks, of the Ohio.

CRIPPLE CREEK (straight harp)

7   6   ⑥   6
I gotta a gal at the head of the creek

5   4   5 ④   4
Going up to see her about 8 times a week.

7   6   ⑥   6
Kiss her on the mouth just as sweet as any wine,

5   4   5 ④   4
Wrap her arms around me like a sweet potato vine.

5   ④ 4 5   6
Goin' up to Cripple Creek, going on a run.

5   ④ 4 5   ④ 4
Goin' up to Cripple Creek to have some fun.

5   ④ 4 5   6
Goin' up to Cripple Creek, going in a whirl.

5   ④ 4 5   ④ 4
Goin' up to Cripple Creek to see my girl.

ON TOP OF OLD SMOKEY (straight harp)

4   5 6 7 ⑥
On top of Old Smokey

⑥ ⑤ 6   ⑥ 6
All covered with snow

4   5 6 ④
I lost my true lover

5 ⑤ 5 4 4
A-courtin' too slow

BILL BAILEY (straight harp)

5   ④   5 ④ 5 6
Won't you come home Bill Bailey,

5 5 ④ 4
Won't you come home?

6   5 6 ⑥ ④
She cried the whole night long,

⑤ 5 ⑤ 5 ⑤ 6 ⑤   5 ⑤
I'll do the dishes, honey, I'll pay the rent.

6   ⑥ 6 5
I know I've done you wrong.

5   ④ 5 ④ 5 6 5   ④ 5
'Member that rainy evening I drove you out,

7   ⑧ 7   ⑥
With nothing but a fine tooth comb?

7   ⑥ 7 8   ⑥
Well I know I'm to blame. Well ain't that a shame,

7 ⑥ 7 ⑥ 8   7
Bill Bailey won't you please come home?

WHEN THE SAINTS GO MARCHING IN (cross harp)

3 ③ 4 ④ 3 ③ 4 ④
Oh when those saints, go marching in,

3 ③ 4 ④ ③ 3 ③ ③
Oh when those saints go marching in.

③ ③3 ③④ 4
Lord, I want to be in that number,

③ 4 ④ ③ 3 ③③
When the saints go marching in.

WHEN THE SAINTS GO MARCHING IN (straight harp)

4 5 ⑤ 6 4 5 ⑤ 6
Oh when those saints, go marching in,

4 5 ⑤ 6 5 4 5 ④
Oh when those saints go marching in.

5 ④ 4 5 6 ⑤
Lord, I want to be in that number,

5 ⑤ 6 5 4 ④ 4
When the saints go marching in.

APPENDIX

TWO

Single Note
Therapy

Problem: You've been at this for a couple of days already and you still can't hit single notes reliably.

Solution: Relax. Nobody can after just a couple of days. Re-read the Single Note Pucker and relax a bit.

Problem: You've been belting out *Clementine* and all the rest for more than a week now, and you still keep getting that blurry sound all the time.

Solution A.: Take your lessons in shorter spurts. One half-hour lesson is less productive than two at 15 minutes each. Your mouth won't get so tired.

Solution B.: Breathe deeply or slowly between riffs or tunes. Slow down the tempo. Say encouraging things to yourself. Massage your chin and mouth. Being tight is not the key.

Solution C.: You can practice the Single Note Pucker even without the harmonica. First, make sure there's no one else in the room, then stand in front of a mirror and look like a fish. (What can I say? That's the way it's supposed to look.) When you're playing, exaggerate this a bit by lowering your jaw and sucking in your cheeks.

THREE

Musical Theory for the Musically Hopeless

Notes and Scales

Music is made up of sounds, or notes. Those that vibrate quickly are higher than those that vibrate slowly.

Notes are organized into scales. In the familiar *do, re, mi, fa, so, la, ti, do,* scale, *do* is lower than *re* is lower than *mi,* is lower than *fa* . . . all the way up to notes that vibrate so fast that only Fido can hear them.

What Key Am I Playing In?

Throughout history, each note has been given a name. The "A" note, "B" note, "C" note, "D" note, "E" note, "F" note, and "G" note. You can start a scale on any of these notes. If you play the *do re mi* scale starting on the note of "A", you are playing in the key of "A". Tunes in this key frequently start and finish on the "A" note, just as tunes in the key of C, generally start and finish on the note of "C".

Chords

For reasons that elude explanation, music obeys laws. The human ear "likes" certain combinations of sounds, and those combinations, it turns out, follow mathematical principals. For example, in a typical scale, if you play the first, third and fifth notes in it, the ear likes that sound. It harmonizes, and we call it a CHORD. If it's the first, third and fifth notes of an A scale, we call it an A chord.

Why Do They Call It a Harmonica?

If you bring your hand down randomly on a set of piano keys, or strum without thinking across the strings of a guitar, the sounds you produce will be discordant, they won't harmonize. But harmonicas are built so that harmonizing notes are arranged side by side. You CAN blow randomly into a set of holes and come up with harmonizing notes.

The Structure of Music

To complete this brief description of the way music comes together, imagine all the chords (A, B, C, D, E, F, and G) arranged into a scale, just like notes. If the guitarist you happen to be accompanying starts a song with an A chord, it's very likely a song played in the key of A. If the starting chord is a D, then it's probably in the key of D.

Theoretically, your guitarist *could* then go to any other chord, but in practice there are patterns that are repeated over and over again.

Let's say your guitarist, playing in the key of A, starts off with an A chord. Since an A note is the first note of the A scale, we'll call the A chord, the "1" chord. The 2 chord is the B chord, the 3 chord is the C chord and so forth.

For reasons that are once again elusive, the ear tends to like a chord progression known as the 1-4-5 progression. In this example, the 4 chord is the D chord, and the 5 chord is the E chord. So the chord progression would go: A to D to E.

If your guitarist is playing in the key of C, beginning with a C chord, he might then go to an F chord next, and then a G chord.

For 25 bonus points, if your guitarist is beginning in the key of D, with a D chord, and if he were going to follow the 1-4-5 progression, what would his next two chords be? *Hint:* Use your fingers.

As a harmonica player, your job is to play patterns of notes that harmonize with the chord progression. These patterns are called riffs, many of which you've learned in this book. Since there are harmonicas built in each key, all you have to do is learn these patterns on one harmonica, in one key, and then you can play in any key.

Incidentally, the answer is G and A.

APPENDIX

FOUR

Advanced Straight Harp

I have a bit of a confession to make. Although much of the emphasis of this book has been on Cross Harp and the power it has with the blues, country and rock and roll, there is also a whole world inside Straight Harp, a world way beyond *Someone's in the Kitchen with Dinah.*

The basic approach to playing improvisational Straight Harp is to accent the blow notes, use the draw notes as Steppingstones and to resolve on 1 blow, 7 blow or 10 blow. This is, you'll note, almost the exact opposite of Cross Harp.

To help keep things straight, the opposite page has a map of the Straight Harp sound.

Here's a simple Straight Harp riff that will always harmonize if you are in tune with the guitarist and are playing the right key of harmonica:

Meadow Lark Melody Run
5 ④ 4.

You can play this same riff on the high as well as low end of your harp 8 ⑧ 7 or 2 ① 1.

These patterns should give you a few ideas for Straight Harp improvisational accompaniment. You can use them as "fillers"— musical phrases that keep a song interesting, or you can use them to create solos. Built on a framework of Straight Harp Harmonizing Notes, the mood and timing of these riffs can be modified to fit the song you're accompanying.

Picking Out Melodies

The only complete scale on your diatonic harp starts on the 4 blow and goes:

4	④	5	⑤	6	⑥	⑦	7
do	re	mi	fa	so	la	ti	do

MAP OF STRAIGHT HARP SYSTEM

10	RESOLUTION
(10)	STEPPING STONE
9	WAILING
(9)	STEPPING STONE
8	WAILING
(8)	STEPPING STONE
7	RESOLUTION
(7)	STEPPING STONE
(6)	STEPPING STONE
6	WAILING
(5)	STEPPING STONE
5	WAILING
(4)	STEPPING STONE
4	RESOLUTION
(3)	STEPPING STONE
3	WAILING
(2)	WAILING
2	WAILING
(1)	STEPPING STONE
1	RESOLUTION

So for a major scale tune (say, for example, that timeless classic *Old MacDonald Had a Farm*) you would probably pick it out on these notes:

7 7 7 6 ⑥ ⑥ 6
Old MacDonald had a farm
8 8 ⑧ ⑧ 7
Eeeeyiiii eeeyiii oooooh

If you tried to pick it out down low, you'd run into a problem with the word "had":

4   4 3 ?   3
Old MacDonald had a farm

The fact is, there isn't a complete scale between holes 1 to 4. Both *fa* and *la* are missing.

But you can finesse the problem by bending 2 and 3 draw, and playing a scale like this:

		bent			bent		
1	**①**	**2**	**②**	**②**	**③**	**③**	**4**
do	*re*	*mi*	*fa*	*so*	*la*	*ti*	*do*

If you can learn this, and it may be the hardest trick in the book, you'll have two complete scales; one between holes 1 and 4, and another between holes 4 and 7.

APPENDIX
FIVE
High Notes

More advanced stuff. Holes 1 through 6 are the heart of Cross Harp play, and they should keep you busy for quite a little while. But eventually, you'll probably want to know something about holes 7 through 10, the upper elevations.

These notes are a bit more difficult to play, but if you've come this far, a little more adversity shouldn't faze you. You'll play more "from your head" for these notes, with a more finely focused airstream.

For your first riff, try the 9 Blow Down. It's exactly like the 6 Blow Down, except up an octave:

The 9 Blow Down

9 ⑨ 8 ⑧ ⑦⑥ 6

Follow that with the 6 Blow Up:

The 6 Blow Up

6 ⑦⑧ 8 9

By now you've probably discovered that 9 blow is not an easy note to hit cleanly.

Practice, practice, practice.

Since everyone needs a goal, I'll give you one: The Complete Blues Scale Up and the Complete Blues Scale Down. If you can play these two with good tone, beat and feeling, then you know your way around a harp.

The Complete Blues Scale Down

9 ⑨ 8 ⑧⑦⑥ 6 ⑤④ ③②

The Complete Blues Scale Up

①2 ②③ 4 ④ 5 6 ⑦⑧ 8 9

APPENDIX
SIX

Open Harp
Surgery

There may come a day when your harp picks up a case of single reed laryngitis that no amount of tapping, blowing, drawing or cursing will cure. Do not despair. Harmonicas are extremely low-tech and respond well to even the feeblest attempts at repair.

With a butter knife, unscrew the top and bottom plates. Try not to lose the screw and nuts. If your problem was in a blow note, look at the reeds exposed under the top plate; if a draw note wouldn't sound, look under the bottom plate. Anything big enough to jam a reed ought to be visible . . . a piece of grit or hair could do it. Dislodge it with your butter knife and put the plates back on.

GLOSSARY

Blow. Blowing into your harmonica.

Draw. Sucking on your harmonica.

Single Note. Playing one note at a time.

Cross Harp. A method of playing blues and country harmonica that accents the draw notes. Good for accompaniment and solo work.

Straight Harp. A method of playing melodies on the harmonica. Accents the blow notes.

Tension. The feeling of anticipation that's characteristic of blues and country music. It's most easily accomplished by playing Cross Harp and accenting the draw notes.

Harmonizing Notes. A single note you can play at any time in a song and know that it will fit. Also known as a Safe Note.

Wailing Note. A Harmonizing Note that creates tension.

Note of Resolution. A Harmonizing Note that resolves tension.

Steppingstone Note. A note that does not harmonize. It's used as a steppingstone between Wailing Notes (which create tension) and Notes of Resolution (which resolve tension).

Blues and Country Harmonica Music. Creating and resolving tension with good tone to a beat.

Riff. Patterns of notes that create and resolve tension and can be used when accompanying guitar, piano or when playing solo.

Harmonica Chord. Three or more Harmonizing Notes played at the same time.

Key. A musical term which identifies the starting and ending place in a song or chord pattern, as in the Key of A, or the Key of D flat.

Tuning. Adjusting the guitar and other instruments to the harmonica.

Bending. Twisting the sound of a single note, making it lower by changing the shape of your mouth.

Frustration. The feeling you get just before you're about to break through into a new level.

More Great Books from **KLUTZ**®

The Book of Classic Board Games

The Buck Book

The Klutz Book of Card Games

The Etch A Sketch Book

Face Painting

Country and Blues Guitar for the Musically Hopeless

Juggling for the Complete Klutz

KidsSongs

KidsSongs 2

KidsSongs Jubilee

KidsSongs Sleepyheads

The Klutz Book of Knots

The Klutz Book of Magic

The Klutz Book of Magnetic Magic

Draw the Marvel™ Super Heroes™

Peg Solitaire

The Rubber Chicken Book

Watercolor for the Complete Klutz

Free Catalogue!

Filled with the entire library of "100% Klutz Certified" books, as well as a diverse collection of other things we happen to like, **The KLUTZ. Catalogue** is, in all modesty, unlike any other catalogue. It's free for the asking!

The KLUTZ. Catalogue
455 Portage Avenue
Palo Alto, CA 94306

(605) 424-0739